Heads   &   Tales

Heads & Tales

THE FILM
PORTRAITS
of
CORNEL
LUCAS

Lennard Publishing 1988

Lennard Publishing

a division of Lennard Books Ltd

Lennard House

92 Hastings Street

Luton, Beds LU1 5BH

British Library Cataloguing in Publication Data

is available for this title

ISBN 1 85291 028 3

First published 1988

© Cornel Lucas 1988

Foreword © David Puttnam 1988

Phototypeset in Perpetua Roman & Italic

by Jigsaw Graphics

Design by Pocknell and Co.

Printed and bound in Great Britain by

Butler & Tanner,

Frome, Somerset.

Photograph of Cornel Lucas

by Fi Magee

CONTENTS

WHENEVER I ASK A photographer to take on the responsibility of shooting the stills for a picture, I always make a point of reminding him (or her) that from ten to one hundred times as many people will see their work as will *ever* see the movie itself. Add to this the fact that many of those who *do* see the film will make their decision based solely on the appeal of the photographs they've seen, and you begin to get some idea of the imagination and skill that's expected of the 'stills man'.

Cornel Lucas is clearly a 'stills man' with golden knobs on! His photographs were seldom used merely as 'lobby cards' or 'front-of-house'. No, Cornel's portraits had a habit of becoming the photographic icons by which we came to know and remember this or that star. Maybe icons is too strong and definitive a word, but I don't think it's misplaced.

For example, if anyone can show me a photograph of Brigitte Bardot (Page 75) which better sums up *exactly* why I fell head over heels in love with her thirty odd years ago, I'll not only be surprised but also eternally grateful!

Was Marlene Dietrich ever better defined in any of the thousands of other images we've seen of her? Or Gregory Peck, or even for that matter, Kate Hepburn? Did Gene Tierney, Petula Clark or Jean Simmons ever look more beautiful? And what was it about those quintessentially English faces of the 40s and 50s, Trevor Howard, Kenneth More and Jack Hawkins that Cornel has captured like no one else?

It's all magic to me, but the greatest moments are not 'glamour' as such, but closer images of cinema itself.

I *love* the portrait of Michael Powell and Emeric Pressburger, and those of Fellini and Huston run it close.

The images of the camera crew on location and the scenic artist suggest another book entirely – but my favourite, without doubt, is the photograph of all of the newsreel cameramen on pages 118-119. Not only a great picture but a summation of an era – without question a legitimate icon in its own right.

Now, with the recent studies of the Waunana Indians, and his 'Archivist's Dream' portraits of award-winning camermen, film editors, art directors, special effects men and the stunning shot of Greta Scacchi, Cornel's work goes from strength to strength, and every frame shows what for me is his outstanding quality, a deep and abiding affection for cinema.

DAVID PUTTNAM

The Image

DAVID ARRIVED unexpectedly at my Chelsea studios just as I was finishing a modelling assignment. Being a great raconteur he told a story of his early modelling days in New York. There, with his new found friend Errol Flynn and two other out-of-work actors, he decided to form the modelling syndicate with a difference. They had noticed, on the few occasions that they had actually found work, how photographers tend to exploit a session. By a rapid change of scenery and props a model could unwittingly be used for several jobs, and yet only receive a single fee. The syndicate decided that each member would be restricted to modelling one part of the body only, a quarter each, head, hands, torso and legs. The first assignment came to Niven. What started as a straightforward trouser shot, soon required him to wear a jacket and be holding a drink. "Not my forte old chap, I'm left handed and feel awkward with a glass in my hand, but give me a moment, I know just the man for the job." Errol got the drink out of that one. It wasn't long before their ploy was discovered, but it was fun while it lasted.

DAVID.NIVEN

1951

VERY OFTEN IT IS not the good photographer in the film studio who gets results, but the good psychologist. On many occasions what I have said to an artist has been more important than what my camera has achieved. However, there is always an incident to prove one wrong, and this happened with Kay Kendall. One of the purposes of the publicity man is to get artists to do things which they really do not want to do.

On this occasion the last thing which Kay Kendall wanted to do was a stills session with me or anyone else. As we were good friends, I was asked to go to her dressing room to attempt to persuade her to do the session. As I approached her room I heard a scream and a clatter. Rushing in, I just caught the end of Kay's dress disappearing out the window. To this day, I am certain that even had the dressing room been on the first floor, she would still have jumped to avoid me.

We met the next day and Kay was her usual charming self. No reference was made to the previous day's excitement.

KAY KENDALL

1952

HOWARD KEEL'S baritone voice sang its way through many well remembered MGM musicals. *Seven Brides for Seven Brothers,* with its zest and unparalleled athletic energy, was one of his hits: so was the 1951 remake of *Showboat,* in which his marvellous voice made the most of some of the greatest songs ever written. At the time of this photograph, he was seeking to break away from the musical mould and switch to straight parts. For this sitting we therefore departed from his usual clean-cut look, for something a little unexpected.

HOWARD KEEL

1957

IT WAS IN 1949 that Jack Warner introduced me to Petula and her father, who was also her manager. During our meeting, her dad made it clear how determined he was that his daughter should break away from the little girl part she was playing in the popular *Huggett* series. He felt she should be playing more mature parts and thought that I could help them by taking some special photographs.

Armed with these photographs, he fought the Front Office and won sympathetic ears. Having served out her apprenticeship, it was not long before her talents as an international performer were acclaimed.

PETULA CLARK

1950

THE ACTOR James Stewart decided to change his name to Stewart Granger, to avoid confusion with the other well known Hollywood actor of the same name. I had worked with Jimmy, as we called him, on a few earlier films, where moments of excitement and tension occurred, but never so much as on one in particular, where the feelings of the star and the male co-star ran so high.

It was apparent during the early rehearsals that neither of them liked each other, and that sooner or later there would be a show-down. The crunch came during a sword fight sequence. Rehearsals had finished, and now the practice foils were replaced with the real weapons. The sequence started when it suddenly became very obvious that they were rapidly moving away from the rehearsed marks. The sequence had been timed for 2 minutes filming, and the director looked very apprehensive when the scene went beyond what had been practised. He shouted "cut! cut" but to no avail. The fight had become real and no longer a film sequence. They battled from one end of the set to the other knocking over things as they went well beyond the set confines. Suddenly it dawned on everybody that this was a genuine fight with no holds barred! The fight had now been going on for 5 minutes with neither side wanting to stop. The director looked a very worried man, for if either actor was injured it would effect the entire film. The finish was quite contrary to the usual where the star always wins.

On this occasion Jimmy received a nasty cut on the arm, and it wasn't until blood had been drawn did they stop! After this episode they both shook hands, and thereafter became good friends.

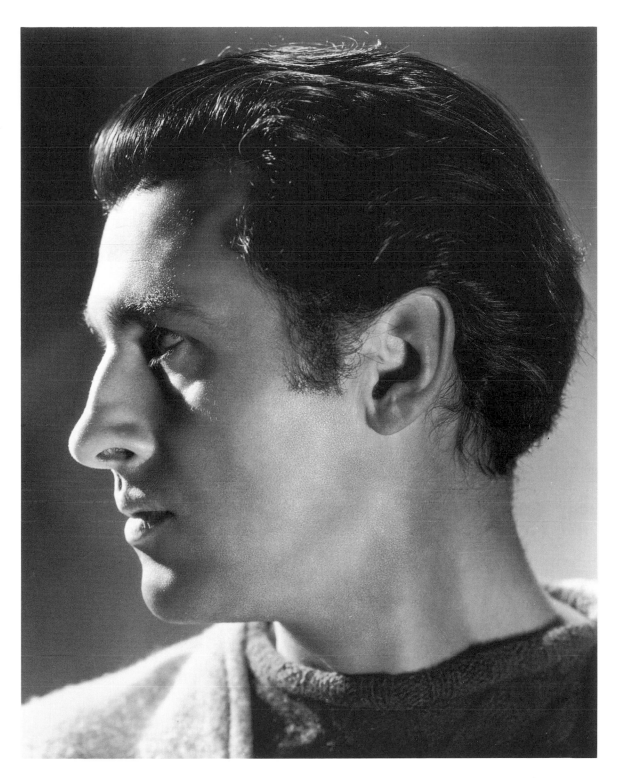

HER FACE WAS referred to as an unmade bed; she said that it was something which she felt quite comfortable in. I wondered what she thought of Twentieth Century Fox erecting a seven storey poster of her: "I'd be happier if it was of the mind and not the body," she mused.

JULIET GRECO

1958

NOT ALL assignments are straight forward – Robert Newton made sure of that. I found him in the bar at Pinewood, a large scotch in one hand and a script in the other. I enquired if he was ready for his session: "You help me to act my part and I'll help you with your photos," he replied.

"But Bob, I'm not an actor," I protested.

"There's always a first time," he said.

So off we went to the most unusual photographic session: my playing Trilby to his Svengali. As time passed, we both came to the same conclusion. Turning to me he said: "I'll stick to acting, Corn, and you take the photo." And that's all I got – one photograph.

ROBERT NEWTON

1955

THE DAY THAT THE most beautiful girl in the world lost confidence in me happened as a result of a swimming sequence.

My job was to capture some off-set pictures of her coming out of the water and to have a courier standing by to dash the negatives to Reuters for global publication. On the morning after the shots, I was summoned by the publicity department to go to see her which I duly did. She told me that the picture which had been published should have been checked first because her mascara had been running down her face and I should have noticed this. I had no excuse and felt obliged to resign. Later in the day when the circumstances of the photographs were explained to her, I was asked to stay on the picture and from that moment on, I became her close friend.

To an actress, the camera has such a critical eye that it demands intense concentration, but at the same time, they require from it just what they want to see. If the results are not to their liking then the performance which they have given has been a poor one. It is up to the photographer to capture that brief moment when satisfaction can be guaranteed.

YVONNE DE CARLO

1952

GRETA WAS A top international model before gracing the big screen. She reminds me of the stars of the 40s and 50s. Her sensitive features, luminous wide-set eyes, straight nose and generous mouth, give her a Garboesque quality. Recently she starred in *White Mischief*, a story of upper class decadence set in Africa, a film in which her beauty was brilliantly captured.

GRETA SCACCHI

1988

DURING THE 50s, money was scarce and neither actors nor technicians earned a great deal. After leaving RADA, my wife's first job was in a small part in the Jean Anouilh play *Jezebel.* The leading man in this Frank Hauser production was Dirk Bogarde.

After the show had finished, on the first pay day, there was a knock at the dressing room door:

"Here you are girls" he said, "I'm sure that you need this more than I do." With this he handed over his earnings for the week, to be shared between Susan and her fellow thespians.

I first met Dirk after his War Service. During those early film years, I was fortunate to photograph him on many occasions. I have always found him an unusually literate and intelligent man.

DIRK BOGARDE

1953

OF THE MANY subjects that I photographed during the 40s and early 50s one artist always stood out, her angular sculptured face shines like a face on a coin where angles of shape signify the person, no half tones are necessary to make known the person. It was usual practice before a photo-session to seek expert advice as to make-up, hair, props etc. Miss Hepburn held herself apart from this type of conventional routine. The only thing she liked to do was to splash her face with crushed ice, to give her skin a glow. No more had to be done as far as she was concerned. I captured this unexpected picture by a lucky chance, catching the eye of Bill the 'Gaffer' (Chief Electrician) who, anticipating my requirement, shone a light from the gantry onto my unsuspecting subject. She was in a mood of contemplation over her lines at the time, and I impulsively took the photograph on my hand-held Rolleiflex. One could never have captured this pose if it had been premeditated and although it is sparsely lit, everyone seeing it recognises that it could be no one else but Katharine Hepburn.

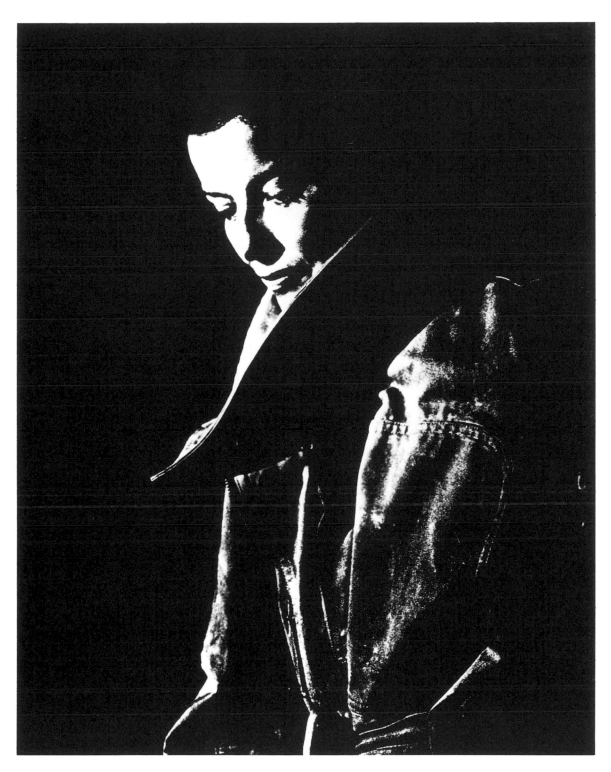

KATHARINE HEPBURN

1950

FAMOUS FOR HIS stage and screen portrayal of Sir Thomas More in *A Man For All Seasons*, I found this most distinguished man unassuming, introspective and a very private person for whom I had the greatest respect. I'm sure these characteristics contribute to the matchless depth he achieves in all his roles. Never known to give less than his best, he is an actor whose film appearances are all too few. I feel that his essential dignity is caught in this portrait.

PAUL SCOFIELD

1959

GLYNIS WAS ONE of my favourites, a true professional and still maintaining a rare sense of humour. I had photographed her many times over the years, then came an interlude whilst she spent some time in Hollywood. The next photograph I took of her was for her Broadway success *A Little Night Music*. It was during this session that she related a lovely story about her experience in Hollywood. It appeared that in the eyes of the Front Office she was the perfect specimen for a physical change and should therefore undergo the Hollywood glamour treatment. After some preliminary photographic sessions, the Front Office explained exactly what changes they required to make to create the perfect visual impact for the camera.

Firstly, they thought that her thighs and buttocks needed more shape and so suggested that all her costumes should have this shape built-in, including room for a ridiculously large bust. She listened in dumb-founded silence as they further required her to cap all her teeth and reshape her eye brows and lip-line, she quickly decided that Hollywood was not for her and soon left for Broadway where she found it was possible to be herself.

GLYNIS JOHNS

1954

A STRANGE MIXTURE of charm and aloofness, a rebel actor and cult hero. His hit TV series *The Prisoner* filmed in the beautiful but unreal village of Port Meirion, gave the 60s audience teasing games and endless puzzles, and still commands a devoted following. In films his intensity has been used to advantage in a number of roles. If one caught him on a bad day he could be silent and uncooperative. I caught him on a good day.

PATRICK McGOOHAN

1 9 5 6

THE AGELESS Cliff Richard has been a pop star since the 50s and is still as popular as ever. In the early 60s, this teenage idol starred in a string of big budget British Musicals. *Summer Holiday,* with Una Stubbs and The Shadows, exactly caught the exuberance of youth, as Cliff and his friends took a London double-decker bus across Europe. It also gave him one of his biggest hit records. *Expresso Bongo,* with the late Laurence Harvey, was an enjoyable look at the music business. At the time of this photograph the young world was Presley crazy. The Elvis look — the sulk, the hair-style — is all here.

CLIFF RICHARD

1960

I HAD SEEN Miss Tierney in Preminger's film *Laura* in 1944. *Laura* was a classic romance, a story of passion and of obsession, and Miss Tierney's appearance was electrifying. Her heart-shaped face was a dream factory creation which had astonishing impact in close-up. When I met her, she was uneasy: her personal life was in turmoil. I felt that silence was the best policy. She was and still remains today a renowned beauty.

GENE TIERNEY

1952

WHILST ATTENDING a small dinner party at the Dorchester I had the pleasure of meeting A.E. Matthews and his wife. During conversation I said that I would very much like to include a portrait of him in a series of pictures of famous people that I was compiling. A.E. agreed, but asked me to ring first. A few weeks later I telephoned him: Who was I, he asked and what did I want? I explained that I was the photographer he had met at the Dorchester a few weeks back and was phoning to arrange to photograph him. To this he replied that if I wanted a picture of him he would send me one! I said that I would come over to collect the photograph and at the same time bring my own camera: this I did. When I arrived at the cottage, I knocked at the door and a voice came forth:

"Who's that?"

"The photographer," I replied.

A head came out of the window above and he informed me that he didn't feel like having his picture taken today and with that he disappeared, banging the window shut. I waited patiently knowing that he would be curious to see whether I had gone. Sure enough he appeared again, and on seeing me said that if I intended to hang around I might as well be of some use: would I go to the pub and buy him a bottle of gin? I agreed to do this if he would let me take his picture. To this, he eventually agreed. When I returned with the gin, he said that he was unable to open the door, so if I wanted to come in, I would have to climb through the window. Fortunately for me his wife then arrived, so such an entrance was unnecessary.

He was wearing a dressing gown and a scarf and said that if he was going to be photographed he would have to put on something more formal, so off he went to change. It was half an hour before he reappeared wearing the same dressing gown, but in place of the scarf, he now wore a tie. He explained that his favourite place for pictures was the kitchen, so amidst all the confusion that was where we worked.

A. E. MATTHEWS

1958

"I WAS NEVER AN actress with a flame," Miss Aimée once said. Ah, but what about this photo? I took this incandescent study at the time she was co-starring with Trevor Howard in a film called *The Golden Salamander.* Big things were expected of her, but they did not come until later, in such films as *La Dolca Vita, 8½, Lola* and *A Man and a Woman.*

ANOUK AIMÉE

1950

LESLIE CARON WAS discovered dancing with Roland Petit's ballet company in Paris by none other than Gene Kelly. The latter announced that he had found the leading lady for his new film *An American In Paris*. Leslie went on to shine in several musicals during the 50s, but wasted no time hanging up her ballet shoes when given the opportunity to act without music. When she came to me, gone was the short gamine haircut: here she is as a reflection of the 60s.

LESLIE CARON

1964

SIR ALEC IS WELL known for his almost chameleon-like ability to play an amazing range of characters. In the Ealing Comedy, *Kind Hearts and Coronets,* he played no less than eight character parts. His other triumphs are far too numerous to mention, but especially memorable was his Herbert Pocket opposite John Mills's Pip in *Great Expectations* and, of course, his Colonel Bogey in *The Bridge on the River Kwai* is one of the finest performances of all time.

This shot for the 1954 romantic comedy *To Paris With Love* shows him as a debonnaire leading man.

SIR ALEC GUINNESS

1954

I WAS ASKED TO photograph Lauren Bacall in the more relaxed and personal atmosphere of her home. I had been warned to expect a person of unpredictable temperament who might need careful handling.

"Good morning Mr. Lucas", was her greeting at the door, "I would like you to take some photographs for the police," and with that she vanished. From that moment on I was prepared for a very unusual session. I waited with nervous anticipation.

"I'm ready!" I looked around to find Miss Bacall's South American cook. I was to take her visa photograph. This completed, Miss Bacall reappeared and I started my second sitting of the morning. I set up my large camera and lights to take typical glossy pictures when Bacall remarked:

"You must be bored of women who want you to make them beautiful all the time. Please would you photograph me just as I am."

This I did on my small camera and then, just for safety's sake, on the large camera too. When I showed her the two quite different final prints she did something that no other actress I have ever photographed had done. She requested that only the unretouched photographs be used.

She told me that ever since she had been a model in New York at the age of sixteen, she had always wanted to look herself. It was this look on the front cover of a Blood Donor magazine that had caused Howard Hawks to have her flown out to Hollywood for a film test at Warner Brothers. When Percy Westmore, the make-up head at Warner's was introduced to her, he explained how he intended to reshape her looks. Her response was to phone up Howard Hawks and beg him to talk to Mr. Westmore. The latter was finally instructed to leave Miss Bacall, with all her so-called blemishes, alone. During the test, she was so nervous that in order to stop herself shaking she had to lower her head. When Howard Hawks viewed the rushes of Bacall's first film, it was decided to adjust the lighting to suit her nervous disposition: this enamoured her even less to Humphrey Bogart, with whom she starred.

LAUREN BACALL

1958

A COLONEL IN charge of ENSA in India during the Second World War, Jack Hawkins returned to become a top box office star of the fifties. He brought dignity and intelligence to all his roles, and was ideally cast as a heroic officer in a number of naval and military films. Many will remember his brilliant performance in *The Cruel Sea* when, as the captain of a beleaguered warship, he had to maintain his courage and equilibrium in the face of relentless adversity. He worked on both sides of the Atlantic and it was a credit to his character that he continued to act, having undergone a serious throat operation in 1965, instead of being content to retire on past glories.

JACK HAWKINS

1953

OVER THE LAST forty years this English Rose has had many successes on both stage and screen. She is perhaps best known for her performances in *A Town Like Alice* and *Carve Her Name With Pride*, Virginia has not only had a brilliant career, but a long and happy marriage to Bill Travers and been a mother to four wonderful children. I admire her enormously.

VIRGINIA McKENNA

1957

TO MY MIND THE most handsome of film stars, but even with his extra-ordinary good looks, he was always rather shy and reticent when it came to gallery portraits. My one ally on these occasions was my Prop man, Ernie Bagley. Calling Peck "Guv'nor", he fed him endless cups of 'char' and told him Cockney jokes which all helped to ease the atmosphere.

Many years later, I learned that the one regular visitor to Ernie's bedside, as he lay dying in St. George's Hospital, was Gregory Peck.

GREGORY PECK

1953

THIS LADY WAS perhaps the greatest female dancer in films and was described by fellow artist Fred Astaire as "beautiful dynamite". Who could forget her seemingly endless legs that danced with faultless precision in *The Bandwagon?* For this Columbia publicity shot, I proposed something different to the usual glamour shots. Instead we achieved a rather jaunty pose with a rakish straw hat. The famous long legs may be clad in casual capris, but the dancer's grace is obvious.

CYD CHARISSE

1966

TREVOR WAS A man full of amusing surprises. On one occasion whilst I was working with him in North Africa, he asked me to join him on a short excursion to a Foreign Legionnaire's fort in the little frequented outpost of Hammamet. He explained that this was where he wanted to build a villa for his eventual retirement. It wasn't until we arrived there that I realized that the villa was to be sited in a portion of even less frequented desert! Nevertheless Trevor happily paid the required deposit of £25 and my role as a witness to the signing of the contract was soon fulfilled.

When I next saw him in Rome during the early 60s I enquired as to whether he had ever built his villa: "I've lost the damned contract and have no intention of retiring!" was his reply.

I FIRST MET Penelope when she was only ten years old. Keen even then to become an actress, she asked my advice:

"I would forget all about acting if I were you," was my emphatic reply. Luckily she ignored me and has recently starred in *Clockwise, Cry Freedom* and many West End plays.

Meeting her recently, I reminded her of the conversation which we had had thirty years ago. Remembering it well she laughed and said: "Corny, I thought you were barmy then and you are just as barmy now."

PENELOPE WILTON

1968

A MOST LIKEABLE leading man of the stage and screen in the 50's, Kenneth More will be forever remembered as a gentle Englishman whose very appearance leant integrity to a film, whether in the pure comedy of *Genevieve,* or nautical roles, as in *A Night To Remember.* All attempts to internationalize him failed, as More was simply too British. This is one of the many portraits I did of him during the making of *Reach For The Sky,* the biographical story of Douglas Bader.

KENNETH MORE

1956

ONE OF THE FEW great stars to emerge in the 60s, Raquel had a wide beauty that captured the mood of her time. From an unforgettable debut, in a prehistoric bikini and speakin gonly a Neanderthal dialect, in *One Million Years BC*, Miss Welch went on to prove her worth in roles that gave her more usual costumers and words. Her TV spectaculars in the early 70s were legendary for their globe-trotting locations and exciting guest stars. I found Raquel a pleasure to photograph, particularly when I suggested that she should remain fully clothed. This sensitive portrait was the result.

RAQUEL WELCH

1974

THIS HUSKY VOICED Italian beauty was an international star in the 60s, featuring notably in films directed by Visconti. For British and American audiences she epitomised the provocative charm of the continental beauty, but her finest work was to be found in the films of the great Italian directors. Paired to startling effect with Burt Lancaster in *The Leopard*, the intensity of her performance was an essential contribution to the genius of that great film. Not as blatantly sexy as some of her contemporaries, in this picture she nevertheless exudes her own unique style and youth.

CLAUDIA CARDINALE

1958

STANLEY WAS ONE of the few British film stars who was truly at home in action roles. He was raised in a Welsh village and was exposed at a very early age to the horrors of unemployment and poverty. Perhaps it was the harsh reality of his childhood which gave him such an assertive character. His forceful nature was present at the age of fourteen, when he appeared in his first dramatic role in *The Druids Rest,* a play by Emlyn Williams. He was the understudy to the then unknown seventeen year old actor, Richard Jenkins, who later changed his name to Burton.

This picture, although showing Stanley in a quiet pose, still conveys a sense of mystery which this Welshman always exuded.

It was a great honour for his family when he was knighted for his outstanding work and contributions to the industry as a whole.

STANLEY BAKER

1955

I FIRST MET JEAN in the make-up room at Pinewood: she was a girl of seventeen. I had been asked to photograph her for a feature in a movie magazine. It was during this session that Jean looked into the mirror: "Corny, I wonder what this face will look like when I'm fifty?" she pondered inquisitively.

"Jeannie, always remember that a woman is responsible for her face at fifty," was my reply. Over the next three years this rising young star occupied a great deal of my working life. She left these shores in 1950 to work under contract in Hollywood for Howard Hughes. She later obtained American citizenship and has remained with Uncle Sam ever since.

JEAN SIMMONS

1 9 4 7

EVERYTHING HAD been arranged when Brigitte phoned to say that she didn't want any more photographs taken: she was exhausted and would be returning to France in a few days. I assured her that my pictures would not take long and that I could convey her youthful sensuality with her fully clothed.

Armed with a bottle of the best champagne, I went to her dressing room. After a few glasses she started giggling and curled up on the floor, looking very much like the sex kitten she was reputed to be. She then agreed to do a brief sitting, during which I noticed that she had a habit of covering her mouth with her hand. When I enquired why, she told me that she felt that her teeth protruded too much, and the more I tried to convince her to the contrary the more self-conscious she became. As the hours wore on and the champagne wore off, I continued to photograph Brigitte until she curled up and fell asleep.

BRIGITTE BARDOT

1955

I FIRST MET Laurence Harvey in Verona in 1953, when he was playing the part of Romeo in Castalani's *Romeo And Juliet*. Harvey had a very busy schedule and unfortunately the planned session coincided with a local heat wave. He arrived dressed as Romeo, but suggested delaying the sitting until the temperature had dropped and in the meantime I was to accompany him around the local markets. I did not realize however, that he intended to go shopping for antiques, still in his Romeo attire. As he was a great spender, the local Italians soon accepted him as another eccentric Englishman.

Laurence Harvey had already made several films by the time I took this photograph. His screen stardom had been acquired in 1958, as the amoral hero in *Room At The Top*. This publicity shot was for the musical *Expresso Bongo*, which co-starred Cliff Richard.

LAURENCE HARVEY

1 9 5 9

I HAVE KNOWN A number of exceptional and beautiful women during my life, but Susan and her mother Linden, with their extraordinarily similar physical characteristics, certainly combine enough grace and beauty to inspire any artist. I met my wife when she was 18 years old, when she was sent down to my studio at Pinewood to be photographed for Rank and Twentieth Century Fox, who wanted to place her under contract.

She thought she could have everything, a career, marriage and at least four children, but it was only a matter of time, before she decided that the last two had the priority – which in fact became a reality.

MY FIRST connection to Jack Buchanan on celluloid was in 1938, when I was first working in the film industry as a junior technician in a laboratory.

I had been allocated the job on the finishing end of a negative processing machine, taking off each reel of film at the right moment.

Sometimes the heat and humidity were very high, and coupled with the monotony, it could make one very drowsy. No single event is more vivid in my mind than falling asleep sitting on a film bin. Whilst I was dozing, little did I know that the film had overrun and was building up on top and around me, until I awoke, reacted in sheer panic and pushed the red stop button. By doing so I ruined whatever film was left in the developing side of the machine.

This caused many scenes of the film *Brewster's Millions* to be ruined. I was fired on the spot but fortunately for me was vindicated as I was really too young for such a responsible job.

I didn't imagine that 18 years later I would be photographing the star of that film, Jack Buchanan. Naturally during the session I mentioned the event, which to my surprise he remembered, but with a difference. He had been told the film had been ruined by fire, which only goes to show that both film and jobs can go up in smoke!

MY FIRST connection to Jack Buchanan on celluloid was in 1938, when I was first working in the film industry as a junior technician in a laboratory.

I had been allocated the job on the finishing end of a negative processing machine, taking off each reel of film at the right moment.

Sometimes the heat and humidity were very high, and coupled with the monotony, it could make one very drowsy. No single event is more vivid in my mind than falling asleep sitting on a film bin. Whilst I was dozing, little did I know that the film had overrun and was building up on top and around me, until I awoke, reacted in sheer panic and pushed the red stop button. By doing so I ruined whatever film was left in the developing side of the machine.

This caused many scenes of the film *Brewster's Millions* to be ruined. I was fired on the spot but fortunately for me was vindicated as I was really too young for such a responsible job.

I didn't imagine that 18 years later I would be photographing the star of that film, Jack Buchanan. Naturally during the session I mentioned the event, which to my surprise he remembered, but with a difference. He had been told the film had been ruined by fire, which only goes to show that both film and jobs can go up in smoke!

JACK BUCHANAN

1955

MISS COLBERT made one silent picture with Frank Capra in 1927, joining Paramount Pictures in 1929, where she played the part of Poppaea, bathing in asses milk, in de Mille's *The Sign of The Cross.*

This outdoor session was a refreshingly different one for Miss Colbert who was keen to be photographed away from the studio. I couldn't help noticing though, that however I attempted to move her, she always returned to the same position. This she did in order to reveal her 'best side'. The seemingly ageless Miss Colbert won an Oscar for her performance in *It Happened One Night,* again directed by Frank Capra.

CLAUDETTE COLBERT

1952

CHRISTENED Marie-Helene, Mlle Demongeot was one of the rising breed of sex kittens of the 50s, when the Monroe influence was everywhere. Mylene was to be out-pouted only by Bardot. She had a hint of mystery in private life and married a French director, the son of Maigret's creator Georges Simenon.

MYLENE DEMONGEOT

1957

DRESSED IN A bright red shirt, Rod burst into my studio:
"My psychiatrist has instructed me to behave just how I feel," he exclaimed.
With that he proceeded to stand on his head!

I was fascinated by this actor's complex personality. I waited until I
thought that the time was right then said: "Rod, I don't suppose we could get
on. I'll join you upside down later."

All aggression gone, he agreed and was a most responsive sitter.

ROD STEIGER

1 9 5 7

"THE BEST THING IN films since Audrey Hepburn" Alec, Guinesss said about her. Susannah York was one of the brightest young actresses ever to come out of RADA. In the early 1960s her gamine English beauty graced a number of films and of course she reached international audiences through *Tom Jones,* Tony Richardson's rumbustuous and earthy frolic through Fielding's classic 18th-century novel. A woman of rare intelligence, Susannah has always held her convictions with fortitude and strength, and the integrity of her character is, I think, well captured in these four studies taken just before her great international success in *Tom Jones.*

SUSANNAH YORK

1 9 6 2

AUSTRALIAN BY birth, the hell-raising Finch was one of the most attractive actors of the British cinema.

Here he is captured in a comparatively reflective mood, complete with a Ronald Colman matinée-idol moustache. I forget exactly why he posed with the typewriter. The glass and cigarette are perhaps more appropriate!

PETER FINCH

1955

DIANA DORS WAS an intelligent woman, as well as being an actress. The Rank organisation, which had 42 artists under contract, found that she above all others tended to be something of an entrepreneur when it came to her own publicity.

I was lucky to be associated with her on two of these memorable occasions. The first was during a Cannes Film Festival. Diana arrived on the Croisette in a blue Cadillac convertible, driven by a blue liveried chauffeur and, to complete the picture, wore a revealing blue dress, with hair to match! That evening she couldn't fail to be anything but the centre of attention. For the public this personified the Dream Factory, and the reaction of the press was to give her world-wide publicity. Diana decided that, from that moment, the winning formula for attracting publicity was to think up some unusual ideas, so she did just that!

During the Venice Film Festival, she appeared on the Lido in a mink bikini. I was privileged to photograph her in this revealing outfit on a gondola. The picture was again given world-wide coverage and helped establish the fact that the British had certainly arrived!

Her late husband and personal manager, Denis Hamilton, also worked on her image. The mischievous alchemy between the two enabled her to establish a reputation that at times up-staged Hollywood. I found Diana a most amusing and talented actress, who brought tears, joy and wonderment into many people's lives, and who possessed a very good sense of humour.

DIANA DORS

1 9 5 4

MARGARET LOCKWOOD has more claim to movie fame than most. She was a stage actress at the age of twelve, made her film debut at eighteen and retired from the screen in 1955, at the age of forty-one. Her greatest film was Alfred Hitchcock's *The Lady Vanishes* in 1938. I took this picture of her when she was appearing in her last stage play *And Suddenly It's Spring*. It shows that retirement did not diminish her beauty and physical allure, which, needless to say, her fans have never forgotten.

MARGARET LOCKWOOD

1972

CASTALANI THE Italian film and theatre director and Howard Hughes had something in common regarding Joan Collins. Both wanted her photographed without make-up – with one she cried, with the other she smiled! After Joan had played many parts in films without doing the kind of work her ability deserved, along came Castalani with a wonderful visual story of William Shakespeare's *Romeo & Juliet*. Whilst Castalani's great wish was to cast Juliet with an unknown or non-actress, Joan felt she could play the part if given the chance. Castalani felt otherwise, but nevertheless agreed to test her after great persuasion on her part. This would not be the usual film test in the studio, but a test in his flat against a simple back drop of a bed sheet and two photo-flood lamps. There would be no sound track, just silent pictures on a 16mm camera. My job was to photograph Joan in a similar manner, after the completion of the test, in order to show, in still form, the characterisation that Castalani had visualised. The first request he made before doing the test was that she should wear no make-up whatsoever, and the second was for her hair to be flattened, and non-existent around her face.

Joan did not expect to be asked to dispense with her two most important assets, which since leaving RADA she'd been given to understand were essential for film actresses to have at all times. What Castalani wanted to see was the face in its full simplicity, with no form of illusion. In fact she looked stunning and to this day retains that foundation that so many women envy, although sadly she didn't get the part.

On another occasion I was asked by Howard Hughes to photograph Joan in a similar fashion, again without make-up and with a polaroid camera. My thoughts went back to the test with Castalani, but to my surprise she accepted the directive with a smile. The pictures were a preliminary before a Hollywood screen test and possible contract with one of the most influential and controversial film makers and this no doubt persuaded her that it was all worthwhile as time has certainly proved!

JOAN COLLINS

1953

THE BRITISH BOY who went to America at the age of four, and who made good the world over. During the austere post-war years, his travels brought him to Berlin for a stage show and these pictures were taken after he came off stage that night. Always a great entertainer, Bob Hope has had a career that has gone from strength to strength.

BOB HOPE

1953

ON THE OCCASION that I photographed Marlene Dietrich I felt very nervous, and had good reason to, with my little experience. I'd heard so much about her technical knowledge, particularly when it came to lighting her face, from which if there was any deviation from her views, there would be trouble.

Into the gates of Denham Studios I drove, taking my portable radio with me, to lend inspiration to what I thought would be a difficult assignment. It was due to take place on one of the main stages, a vast space, bare apart from a 12′ × 10′ photographic backdrop. I thought this rather underdressed, considering the stage itself measured 300′ × 150′. I turned my radio on to give the place a little atmosphere and on came the great lady, followed by her publicity director, secretary, dresser, make-up and hair girls and finally the producer, all in single file behind her. I suddenly realized the music coming over the radio was *Colonel Bogie* and that they all seemed to be marching in time to it. As they reached me I turned the radio off, but she roared with laughter, saying "I can see you have a good sense of humour, let's start work".

MARLENE DIETRICH

1948

WHEN I MET Richard Burton he had just made a stage success at Oxford and, as usual on all these occasions, film casting directors were keen to recruit a talented young actor. I was asked to prepare a series of photographs of him. We met in the bar at Pinewood to discuss the session, but were suddenly interrupted by a secret message from publicity to the effect that the executive producer wanted to talk to me. Off I went, to be told that Burton's complexion was too coarse for the movie screen. I was to cancel the session.

I returned to the bar and explained as best I could that our intended session·had been temporarily cancelled. Smiling brightly as he left, he said:

"Ah well, if things don't go well with the acting I can always go back to the mines."

RICHARD BURTON

1951

'THE ONE WHO

GOT AWAY'

The Image Makers

Frozen in a scene from the film **The Red Shoes,** *Powell and Pressburger's exquisite celebration both of ballet and the demands it places on its performers.*

M O I R A S H E A R E R &

R O B E R T H E L P M A N N

1 9 4 7

My first meeting with Emeric Pressburger and Michael Powell came when I was assigned to take some special photographs of the famous **Red Shoes** Ballet sequence. It was during this time that Emeric and I became close friends. He could tell the most interesting stories while translating his thoughts from his native Hungarian to English: this required absolute concentration on the part of the listener. The pleasure of one of his stories has remained with me over the years.

As a protégé of his compatriot Alexander Korda, he was asked, whilst at Denham Studios, to look at an espionage thriller which Korda thought contained the perfect role for Conrad Veidt. At the time, Veidt was to make three films for Korda but only if the scripts met with the former's approval. For some reason even Korda, who had a most persuasive personality, could not entice Veidt to do this particular story. Emeric agreed to look at the script to see if he could make it more attractive to Veidt. The plot was dramatic and had a good beginning, middle and end. However, Emeric's essentially foreign eye, after the first reading, pin-pointed Veidt's uneasiness with the script. **The Spy In Black**, presently scripted for a woman as the lead part, should of course be played by a man!

When Veidt read the amended version he immediately identified himself in the new leading role, and agreed to star in the film. From that moment on the partnership of Pressburger & Powell was sealed.

EMERIC PRESSBURGER &
MICHAEL POWELL 1985.

In the early 30s, my brother, who was working in the film industry, took me on a brief visit to the studios. It was on this occasion that I caught sight of the young Anthony Asquith, accompanied by the movie star Gloria Swanson, who was then working on the only film she ever made in this country. This chance experience had a lasting effect on me. The next opportunity that I had to meet Anthony Asquith was some twenty years later, when he was directing **The Browning Version** *and he kindly agreed to come to my studio for this study.*

ANTHONY ASQUITH

1951

During the filming of **8½** at Cinnecitta studios in Rome, I was amazed to see Fellini cracking a 15ft whip, like a circus trainer, whilst giving out directions to Marcello Mastroianni and the rest of the cast. Here the ringmaster glares away from my untamed lens.

FEDERICO FELLINI

1963

*Having made an unforgettable
impression on cinema goers as the
naive and violent thug in the film
of Graham Greene's **Brighton
Rock**, Richard Attenborough
soon put his talents to work on the
other side of the camera. I have
known 'Dickie' as an actor, and
now as a Producer/Director, for a
very long time. He has the
durability of a hardened
professional, surviving to
establish himself as the 'Head
Boy' of British films today.*

*When I photographed him
he was in excellent spirits, as he
had recently acquired the
necessary finance to secure the
making of his film **Gandhi.** A
dream of his for over twenty years,
Gandhi was a project that
required all his strength and
integrity to bring to the screen
and the results were well worth
the wait. Blessed with this news
and coupled with Dickie's copious
experience on both sides of the
camera, the session flowed
smoothly.*

SIR RICHARD ATTENBOROUGH

1982

Of all movie directors, the face that constantly attracted me, with its hard-earned lines and warm twinkling eyes, was that of John Huston. The son of the great character actor, Walter Huston, John's career was both as director and as an actor. In the 50s, he came to Britain to direct one of his greatest films, **Moby Dick**, filmed with extraordinary attention to the use of delicate colour, and still admired for the technical expertise of the great white whale itself. It was a film that gave Gregory Peck, in Captain Ahab, a role of depth and mystery. As an actor John Huston was never better than when he played the corrupt millionaire in **Chinatown**, a part that mixed evil and charisma to great effect.

This part was of course quite uncharacteristic of John Huston the man. I photographed him shortly before he died, when, although in a wheelchair and needing oxygen, he gave me his time most unselfishly.

JOHN HUSTON

1987

In spite of the fact that David Lean was brought up as a Quaker, and was not allowed to visit the cinema, he went on to become one of the greatest film directors of this century. His mastery of terror and tension, and his ability to draw the very best out of his entire cast, were both brilliantly realised in **Great Expectations**, a film which still influences all serious directors. His interest in the epic and heroic gave us two of the finest celebrations of English manhood ever filmed, **Lawrence of Arabia** and **The Bridge on the River Kwai.**

During my session he asked me if I could remember the famous picture of Churchill taken during the war by Karsh. He then assumed a similar pose and this was the result.

SIR DAVID LEAN

1987

This formal picture was taken during the period when David was busy leading the vanguard of the British invasion of Hollywood, with such brilliant films as **Chariots of Fire** *and* **The Killing Fields.**

The son of a respected Fleet Street photographer, David has always shown a keen interest in the art of photography. Having spent a short time in Hollywood, he is now back with many British projects in hand.

DAVID PUTTNAM

1983

*Even in Chelsea, it must have seemed an odd sight on a cold winter's evening to see this unlikely trio descend from a car, carrying their weapons of war, their faces ablaze with paint. They had been flown to London by Enigma Productions on a special assignment for the film **The Mission**.*

Outside their homeland for the first time, the sun now replaced by the intense glare of the studio lights, their look of bewilderment was unmistakeable as I presented them with the preliminary polaroids taken only seconds before. With the help of an interpreter from the Columbian embassy, I managed to complete this unusual study, and so release these hunters of the Waunana tribe back to the jungle which was their only home.

SUMMER IN COLUMBIA,
WINTER IN LONDON

*It is so rarely appreciated that scenic artists create the **look** of a film: the castle walls, the apartment, the street scene, are almost always created on the set. Here a scenic artist is seen at work.*

SCENIC ARTIST

1950

These men risk their lives doing the stunts that we are made to believe the stars perform. They are a special breed of men who direct themselves, and make a very important contribution to the finished film.

STUNT ARTIST

1950

One of the many expert craftsmen
of the Film Industry.

PANICHELLE
(MASTER PLASTERER)
1956

The British producer Castleton
Knight could be regarded as the
Cecil B. de Mille of newsreel. One
day in 1952 he asked if I could
photograph the team of
cameramen assembled to cover the
Derby. The group (including such
companies as Gaumont-British
News, Paramount and British
Movietone) all met at dawn on the
day of the big race. I took this
now-historic picture, a document
of a splendid breed of news
coverage men — soon to be
replaced by television.

NEWSREEL CAMERAMEN

1 9 5 2

Back Row *(L to R):*
Chris Menges, Billy Williams,
Douglas Slocombe,
Ronnie Taylor, Arthur Ibbitson,
the late John Alcott,
Jack Hildyard and
Freddie Francis.

Front Row *(L to R):*
Gerry Turpin, Jack Cardiff,
Guy Green, Freddie Young,
Ossie Morris and
Chris Challis.

AWARD WINNING

DIRECTORS OF

PHOTOGRAPHY

Back Row *(L to R):*
Tony Gibbs, Ralph Sheldon,
Tony Ham, Gerry Hamoling,
Ralph Kempling, Bill Blunden
and Dick Marden.

Front Row *(L to R):*
Ann Cherwadden,
Tom Priestley, Jim Clark,
John Bloom, Mike Bladsell
and Ann Coates.

AWARD WINNING

FILM EDITORS

Back Row *(L to R):*

Ken Adam, Robert Laing,

Roy Walker, Terry Marsh,

Robert Lange, Stuart Craig

and Les Dilley.

Front Row *(L to R):*

Carmen Dillon, John Box,

Michael Seymour and

Norman Reynolds.

AWARD WINNING

FILM ART

DIRECTORS

(L to R): George Gibbs, John Stears, Kit West, Charles Staffell, Brian Johnson, Roy Field, Derek Meading and Richard Conway.

AWARD WINNING

SPECIAL EFFECTS

MEN

When one considers how much time this man has given to the cinema it is remarkable. There are very few people in the movie business who have won 3 Oscars and have been in the Industry for over 70 years.

He is a veteran of the finest quality, an unpretentious man who has collected on his way a number of good friends, and I am privileged to think that I am one of them.

F R E D D I E   Y O U N G

D I R E C T O R   O F

P H O T O G R A P H Y   1 9 8 3

Movie Team shooting in the Pacific Ocean.

MOVIE CAMERAMEN

1948

Technical Notes

Until my departure from the film industry in 1959, I took my pictures on Kodak 10x8 and 7x5 plate cameras on Super XX cut film. I left as the Star Promotion System came to a close, and the established glamour portrait was no longer required. The new Independent Companies concentrated more on the smaller format cameras and with their arrival I said farewell to the star system as I had known it.

ACKNOWLEDGEMENTS:

I dedicate this book to the back-room boys and girls. The processing, printing, retouching and finishing, make-up, hairdressing, wardrobe, and publicity: all those who helped me to capture these images from the past.

I am grateful to the artists, directors and producers whose encouragement and co-operation enabled me to work in their 'Dream Factory'.

Special thanks to the Rank Organisation, Universal/International Pictures and Columbia Pictures for giving me the wonderful opportunity to work with such talented people during the most exciting period of film making.

To the following people I would like to express particular appreciation: Cyril Howard, Managing Director of Pinewood Studios; Sid and Gordon of Pinewood Stills Department; Mrs Joyce Bland, my retoucher over the years; and most of all my dear wife Susan, who not only brought her personal beauty to one of the pages of this book, but was a constant help and guidance.

STARS OF TODAY

I wonder if, in 30 years time, people will still talk of the stars of today in the same way that our mothers and fathers spoke of Valentino, Fairbanks, Garbo and Dietrich, and the dreams they inspired – perhaps not.

I think that television is rapidly stifling our imagination. We are brought too close to the factory of dreams – mystery and enchantment vanish with such familiarity.